Luca Petrov

Greece
Travel Guide

© 2023 Luca Petrov. All rights reserved.
Images Source:
Pixbay: (https://pixabay.com/)
All images' rights belong to their respective owners.
For detailed copyright and disclaimer, kindly visit the last page of this book.

Catalog

Welcome to Greece 1
    Cultural Odyssey 1
    Hellenic Elegance 3
    Kali Orexi 3
    Diverse Landscapes 4
Top 24 Must-Visit Destinations of Greece 5
    1. Athens: 5
    2. Santorini: 6
    3. Crete: 7
    4. Delphi: 8
    5. Thessaloniki: 9
    6. Meteora: 10
    7. Rhodes: 11
    8. Nafplio: 12
    9. Olympia: 12
    10. Mykonos: 13
    11. Corfu: 14
    12. Delos: 15
    13. Monemvasia: 15
    14. Skiathos: 16
    15. Zakynthos: 17
    16. Mycenae: 18
    17. Hydra: 19
    18. Kalamata: 20
    19. Patmos: 21
    20. Ithaca: 21
    21. Epidaurus: 22
    22. Aegina: 23
    23. Naxos: 24
    24. Kastoria: 25
Essential Information 26
First Time in Greece? 30
    What to Wear: 30
    Sleeping: 30
    What to Pack: 30
    Money: 31
    Etiquette: 32
Itineraries 33
    Aegean Odyssey - 2 Weeks 33

- Island-Hopping Extravaganza - 3 Weeks 33
- Mainland Marvels - 2 Weeks 34
- Peloponnesian Passage - 1 Week 34

Food and Drinks 35
- The Gastronomic Calendar 35
- Affordable Delights 36
- Adventurous Tastes 38
- Local Culinary Treasures 38

Adventure Activities Across Greece 40
- Hiking 40
- Cycling 42
- Skiing 42
- Diving 43
- White-Water Sports 44
- Rock Climbing 44
- Sailing 45
- Windsurfing 46
- Best Times to Go 47

A brief History of Greece 48

Other Useful Information 55
- Accommodation in Greece 55

1. Booking Strategies: 55
2. Seasonal Rate Dynamics: 55
3. Location-Driven Pricing: 55
4. Meal Packages and Board Options: 56
5. Bargaining Strategies: 56
- Accommodation Types in Greece: 56

1. Boutique Guesthouses (Pensioni): 56
2. Camping Adventures: 56
3. Monastic Retreats: 57
4. Youth Hostels (Ostelli per la Gioventù): 57
5. Hotels and Pensions: 57
6. Mountain Hut Retreats: 57
7. Rental Accommodations: 57
8. Seaside Villas: 58
9. Government Accommodation Tax: 58
- Customs Regulations in Greece 58
- Navigating Finances in Greece 60
- Public Holidays in Greece 63
- Telecommunication Insights for Greece 63
- Visas and Residency in Greece 64

Travelling to Greece 65
Getting Around Greece 67

Welcome to Greece

Cultural Odyssey

Greece: A Tapestry of History and Myth

While Paris may hold its charm, Greece boasts cities that stand as testaments to a rich historical and mythical legacy. Athens, Thessaloniki, and Crete are among the gems that unveil Greece's cultural tapestry, resonating with tales from ancient civilizations. As the birthplace of democracy and a hub for philosophy, Greece invites you to explore the cradle of Western civilization.

Athens: The City of Wisdom and Ruins

Athens, known as the City of Wisdom, invites you to wander through the ruins of the Acropolis, where the Parthenon proudly stands. Dive into the National Archaeological Museum to discover artifacts that weave tales of gods and heroes, bringing Greek mythology to life.

Thessaloniki: A Cultural Crossroads

Thessaloniki, a vibrant coastal city, is a crossroads of cultures. Explore the White Tower, an emblem of the city, and the Rotunda, a monument with a storied past. As you stroll through the historic Ano Poli district, centuries of history unfold in narrow streets and Byzantine walls.

Crete: Mythical Isles and Minoan Wonders

Crete, the largest Greek island, offers more than sun-drenched beaches. Unearth the mysteries of the ancient Minoan civilization at the Palace of Knossos. The myth of the Minotaur and the Labyrinth comes alive as you traverse the archaeological marvels of this enchanting island.

Hellenic Elegance

In Greece, the intertwining of life and art is an age-old dance. From the verses of Homer to the philosophies of Aristotle, Greece has fostered a legacy that extends beyond its ancient roots. Yet, it is also a modern haven for contemporary artists, visionary chefs, and architectural innovators like Santiago Calatrava.

The Greek spirit cherishes life's finer moments, from the rhythmic steps of traditional dances to the aroma of souvlaki sizzling on open grills. Embrace the ethos of "kefi," an exuberance for life that echoes through lively tavernas, street markets, and the warmth of local hospitality.

Kali Orexi

Greece, a land that whispers culinary tales, is more than a feast for the senses. Indulge in the symphony of flavors, from moussaka to baklava, each dish a revelation of tradition and innovation. Greek cuisine, rooted in fresh and seasonal ingredients, transcends rustic simplicity to achieve culinary brilliance.

Embark on a gastronomic journey through the narrow alleys of Plaka in Athens, savoring mezedes and local wines. Explore the seafood delights of Thessaloniki's Modiano Market or lose yourself in the olive groves of Crete, where the golden elixir of extra virgin olive oil awaits.

Diverse Landscapes

Beyond its cultural riches, Greece unfolds a landscape that captivates with its diversity. From the towering peaks of Mount Olympus to the azure waters of the Aegean Sea, Greece beckons explorers to embrace both the tranquil and the adventurous.

Ski down the slopes of Parnassos, traverse the Samaria Gorge in Crete, or sail through the Cyclades, where whitewashed villages cling to cliffs. Greece's natural wonders promise a journey through landscapes as varied as its mythological tales, inviting outdoor enthusiasts to discover the country's untamed beauty.

Top 24 Must-Visit Destinations of Greece

1. Athens:

- **General Details:** Athens, the cradle of democracy, intertwines ancient marvels with a lively modern spirit. The Acropolis, an enduring symbol, crowns the city, showcasing the Parthenon and ancient Agora. In the historic Plaka district, narrow streets lead to charming cafes and traditional tavernas. Vibrant street art contrasts with classical monuments, embodying a city that bridges the gap between antiquity and contemporary energy. Visit in spring or fall for milder weather, exploring this dynamic metropolis where history resonates on every corner.

- **Key Attractions:** Acropolis, Parthenon, Ancient Agora.

- **When to Visit:** Best from March to May and September to November to avoid extreme temperatures.

- **Opening Hours**: Acropolis: 8:00 AM - 8:00 PM (Varies seasonally).

- **Contact Info**: +30 210 3214172, [Official Website](https://www.theacropolismuseum.gr/en)

- **Hidden Gems:** Anafiotika, a charming neighborhood resembling a Greek island village within the city.

2. Santorini:

  - **General Details:** Santorini, a Cycladic gem, bathes in the Aegean's azure embrace. Famous for its captivating sunsets over the caldera, Santorini's white-washed buildings cling to volcanic cliffs. Explore Oia's narrow alleys, relax on Red Beach, and savor local cuisine in traditional tavernas. May to October offers ideal weather. Witness the island's unique beauty, where ancient history meets Instagram-worthy panoramas, creating an unforgettable tapestry.
  - **Key Attractions:** Oia Sunset, Fira, Red Beach.
  - **When to Visit:** April to October for warm weather and vibrant atmosphere.
  - **Contact Info:** No specific contact for the island.
  - **Hidden Gems:** Pyrgos Village, a less crowded spot with a medieval castle.

3. Crete:

- **General Details:** Crete, Greece's largest island, unfolds a tapestry of diverse landscapes and ancient tales. The Palace of Knossos reveals Minoan grandeur, while the Samaria Gorge beckons hikers. Chania's Venetian charm and Rethymno's Ottoman influences add cultural depth. Best explored from May to September, Crete invites you to taste Cretan hospitality, swim in crystal-clear waters, and immerse yourself in a blend of mythology and vibrant traditions.
- **Key Attractions**: Palace of Knossos, Samaria Gorge, Chania Old Town.
- **When to Visit:** May to September for beach weather and outdoor activities.
- **Opening Hours:** Palace of Knossos: 8:00 AM - 8:00 PM.

- **Contact Info:** +30 2810 231940, [Official Website](https://www.heraklionmuseum.gr)
- **Hidden Gems:** Elafonissi Beach, known for pink sand and crystal-clear waters.

4. Delphi:

- **General Details:** Delphi, perched on Mount Parnassus, echoes with whispers of ancient prophecies. Home to the Oracle of Delphi, it boasts the Temple of Apollo and a theater overlooking the valley. Explore in spring or autumn to enjoy mild weather. The mystical aura of this UNESCO site, once considered the center of the world, invites contemplation amid ancient ruins, revealing the spiritual heart of classical Greece.

- **Key Attractions:** Temple of Apollo, Ancient Theater, Oracle of Delphi.
  - **When to Visit:** Spring or autumn to avoid extreme heat.
  - **Opening Hours:** Archaeological Site: 8:00 AM - 8:00 PM.
  - **Contact Info:** +30 2265 083210, [Official Website](https://www.delphi.gr)
  - **Hidden Gems:** Tholos of Athena Pronaia, a circular temple less frequented.

5. Thessaloniki:

  - **General Details:** Thessaloniki, Greece's cultural capital, unfolds along the Thermaic Gulf. The White Tower and Rotunda stand as testaments to its rich history. Ano Poli's labyrinthine streets reveal Byzantine secrets. Spring and fall offer ideal weather for exploring archaeological treasures and experiencing the city's dynamic arts scene. From the vibrant markets to waterfront cafes, Thessaloniki effortlessly merges tradition with a youthful spirit, creating a tapestry of Greek life.
  - **Key Attractions**: White Tower, Rotunda, Ano Poli.
  - **When to Visit:** Spring and fall for mild weather and cultural events.

- **Contact Info:** +30 231 266 4433, [Official Website](https://www.thessaloniki.travel)
- **Hidden Gems:** Navarinou Square, a vibrant hub for local cafes and street art.

6. Meteora:

- **General Details:** Meteora, a celestial rock forest in central Greece, rises dramatically, crowned by monasteries defying gravity. A UNESCO World Heritage site, Meteora's spiritual energy invites contemplation. Best explored from May to October, the network of trails leads to breathtaking views. Varlaam and Great Meteoron monasteries reveal Byzantine artistry amid natural wonders. This ethereal landscape, suspended between earth and sky, promises a unique pilgrimage into Greece's spiritual heart.
- **Key Attractions:** Varlaam Monastery, Great Meteoron Monastery, Theopetra Cave.
- **When to Visit:** May to October for the best weather.
- **Opening Hours**: Varies by monastery; generally 9:00 AM - 4:00 PM.
- **Contact Info**: +30 2432 022414, [Official Website](http://www.meteora.com)

- **Hidden Gems:** The hiking trails around Meteora for stunning views.

7. Rhodes:

   - **General Details**: Rhodes, a Dodecanese jewel, unfolds layers of history within its medieval walls. The Palace of the Grand Master in Rhodes Town transports visitors to the knights' era. Pristine beaches and Lindos Acropolis beckon exploration. Visit from April to October for warm weather. Whether strolling through the Old Town's cobbled streets or relaxing on sun-soaked shores, Rhodes captivates with its timeless charm.
   - **Key Attractions:** Palace of the Grand Master, Old Town, Lindos Acropolis.
   - **When to Visit**: April to October for warm weather.
   - **Opening Hours:** Palace of the Grand Master: 8:00 AM - 8:00 PM.
   - **Contact Info:** +30 2241 022259, [Official Website](https://www.rhodes.gr)
   - **Hidden Gems**: Seven Springs, a serene oasis surrounded by lush vegetation.

8. Nafplio:

- **General Details**: Nafplio, a romantic seaport town, whispers tales of Venetian and Ottoman influences. Cobbled streets wind around the Palamidi Fortress, offering panoramic views. Best explored in spring or early autumn, Nafplio's charm lies in its historic squares, waterfront cafes, and the Bourtzi Castle. This Peloponnesian gem invites visitors to lose themselves in a timeless ambiance.
- **Key Attractions**: Palamidi Fortress, Bourtzi Castle, Nafplio Old Town.
- **When to Visit:** Spring and early autumn for pleasant weather.
- **Contact Info:** +30 2752 027051, [Official Website](http://www.nafplio.gr)
- **Hidden Gems:** Arvanitia Promenade, a scenic coastal walk.

9. Olympia:

- **General Details:** Olympia, where the spirit of athletic competition once soared, remains the cradle of the ancient Olympic Games. The Temple of Zeus and the ancient stadium echo the cheers of long-past spectators. Best visited from April to June or September, the archaeological site invites travelers to immerse themselves in the birthplace of Olympism, connecting with history amid serene surroundings.
- **Key Attractions:** Temple of Zeus, Ancient Stadium, Archaeological Museum.
- **When to Visit**: April to June and September for milder temperatures.
- **Opening Hours**: Archaeological Site: 8:00 AM - 8:00 PM.
- **Contact Info:** +30 2624 022209, [Official Website](https://www.olympia-greece.org)
- **Hidden Gems:** Philippeion, a circular memorial dedicated to Philip II of Macedon.

10. Mykonos:

- **General Details:** Mykonos, a Cycladic playground, invites revelry amid charming white-washed streets. Little Venice's seaside cafes and iconic windmills define the island's allure. Best enjoyed from May to October, Mykonos pulsates with energy day and night. From lively beach clubs to the tranquility of

Armenistis Lighthouse, the island captivates with its vibrant contrasts.
   - **Key Attractions:** Little Venice, Mykonos Windmills, Psarou Beach.
   - **When to Visit:** May to October for the lively atmosphere.
   - **Contact Info**: No specific contact for the island.
   - **Hidden Gems:** Armenistis Lighthouse for panoramic views.

11. Corfu:

   - **General Details:** Corfu, an Ionian gem, unfolds its Venetian charm against a backdrop of olive groves and turquoise waters. Corfu Town's narrow alleys lead to the Achilleion Palace and hidden gems like Angelokastro. Ideal from May to October, Corfu invites exploration of both historic landmarks and pristine beaches, creating a harmonious blend of nature and culture.
   - **Key Attractions:** Corfu Town, Achilleion Palace, Paleokastritsa Monastery.
   - **When to Visit:** May to October for warm weather.
   - **Contact Info:** +30 2661 313022, [Official Website](https://www.corfu.gr)
   - **Hidden Gems**: Angelokastro, a Byzantine castle with spectacular views.

12. Delos:

- **General Details:** Delos, a sacred isle near Mykonos, stands as an open-air museum of ancient wonders. The Terrace of the Lions and the House of Dionysus reveal its mythical past. Explore from April to October, as this UNESCO site beckons with the echoes of ancient ceremonies and the grandeur of a bygone era.
- **Key Attractions:** Terrace of the Lions, House of Dionysus, Temple of Isis.
- **When to Visit:** April to October when the site is open.
- **Opening Hours:** 8:00 AM - 3:00 PM (varies by season).
- **Hidden Gems:** The ancient theater, where performances were held to honor the gods.

13. Monemvasia:

- **General Details:** Monemvasia, a medieval fortress town, emerges from the rock like a forgotten dream. Cobbled streets, ancient churches, and the imposing Monemvasia Castle transport visitors to a time long past. Best visited in spring or autumn, this hidden gem invites exploration of its Byzantine and Venetian heritage, revealing layers of history on every stone.
- **Key Attractions:** Monemvasia Castle, Church of Elkomenos Christos, Agia Sophia.
- **When to Visit:** Spring and autumn for milder temperatures.
- **Contact Info:** +30 2732 061268, [Official Website](http://www.monemvasia.gr)
- **Hidden Gems:** Lazareto, a historic site on the island of Gefyra.

14. Skiathos:

- **General Details:** Skiathos, a verdant gem in the Northern Sporades, enchants with its golden beaches and lively atmosphere. Koukounaries Beach and Skiathos Town pulse with energy. Best enjoyed from May to October, the island's diverse landscape, from Kastro's ancient ruins to the tranquil beauty of Kastro Beach, promises an unforgettable Greek escape.
- **Key Attractions:** Koukounaries Beach, Skiathos Town, Banana Beach.
- **When to Visit**: May to October for beach weather.

- **Hidden Gems:** Kastro, an ancient fortress with panoramic views.

15. Zakynthos:

   - **General Details:** Zakynthos, an Ionian paradise, boasts not only Shipwreck Beach and Blue Caves but also a rich cultural tapestry. May to October unveils the island's splendor. From the iconic Navagio to the charming Zakynthos Town, the island invites exploration, blending natural wonders with vibrant local life.
   - **Key Attractions**: Shipwreck Beach, Blue Caves, Zakynthos Town.
   - **When to Visit:** May to October for warm weather.
   - **Contact Info:** No specific contact for the island.
   - **Hidden Gems:** Keri Lighthouse, offering panoramic views of the island.

16. Mycenae:

- **General Details:** Mycenae, a testament to ancient greatness, reveals the grandeur of the Mycenaean civilization. The imposing Lion Gate and the Treasury of Atreus stand as iconic landmarks. Best explored from April to October, this archaeological site offers a journey into the past, where myths and reality intertwine amid well-preserved ruins.
- **Key Attractions:** Lion Gate, Treasury of Atreus, Mycenae Archaeological Museum.
- **When to Visit:** April to October for pleasant weather.
- **Opening Hours:** Archaeological Site: 8:00 AM - 8:00 PM.
- **Contact Info:** +30 2751 076742, [Official Website](http://odysseus.culture.gr)
- **Hidden Gems:** Grave Circle A, a burial site with impressive artifacts.

17. Hydra:

- **General Details:** Hydra, a Saronic jewel, captivates with its car-free charm and preserved architecture. Hydra Town's elegant simplicity and Vlichos's quiet fishing village create a serene atmosphere. Best visited from April to October, the island's timeless beauty, from Kamini's tranquility to the artistic allure of Hydra Museum Historical Archives, invites leisurely exploration.
- **Key Attractions:** Hydra Town, Hydra Museum Historical Archives, Kamini.
- **When to Visit:** April to October for a lively atmosphere.
- **Hidden Gems:** Vlichos, a quiet fishing village with traditional tavernas.

18. Kalamata:

- **General Details:** Kalamata, a seaside haven in the Peloponnese, unfolds its history through landmarks like Kalamata Castle. The historic center, with its traditional architecture, invites exploration. Best enjoyed from April to June or September to October, Kalamata's culinary delights, from seaside tavernas to the Kalamata Dance Megaron, offer a delightful taste of Greek life.

- **Key Attractions:** Kalamata Castle, Benakeion Archaeological Museum, Kalamata Main Square.

- **When to Visit:** April to June and September to October for pleasant weather.

- **Contact Info:** +30 2721 227292, [Official Website](http://www.kalamata.gr)

- **Hidden Gems:** Kalamata Dance Megaron, showcasing traditional Greek dance.

19. Patmos:

- **General Details**: Patmos, a sacred Dodecanese isle, unveils spiritual wonders in the Cave of the Apocalypse and the Monastery of Saint John the Theologian. Best visited from May to September, the island's tranquility extends to hidden gems like Petra Beach, inviting contemplation amid nature's beauty.
- **Key Attractions:** Cave of the Apocalypse, Monastery of Saint John, Skala Village.
- **When to Visit:** May to September for warm weather.
- **Contact Info:** +30 2247 031322, [Official Website](https://www.patmos.gr)
- **Hidden Gems:** Petra Beach, a tranquil spot away from the crowds.

20. Ithaca:

- **General Details**: Ithaca, the mythical home of Odysseus, exudes tranquility and timeless beauty. Vathi's picturesque harbor and Anogi's authentic village life showcase the island's diversity. Best explored from May to October, Ithaca's hidden gem, Dexa Beach, offers a secluded retreat amid crystal-clear waters and serene landscapes.
  - **Key Attractions:** Vathi, Odysseus Statue, Anogi Village.
  - **When to Visit:** May to October for pleasant weather.
  - **Hidden Gems**: Dexa Beach, a secluded spot with crystal-clear waters.

21. Epidaurus:

- **General Details**: Epidaurus, famed for its ancient theater, allows visitors to step into history. Witness performances in the well-preserved amphitheater, surrounded by the lush landscape. Best visited from April to October, Epidaurus reveals its ancient healing center, the Sanctuary of Asklepios, and the intriguing Tholos, creating a unique blend of culture and nature.
  - **Key Attractions:** Ancient Theater of Epidaurus, Sanctuary of Asklepios, Archaeological Museum of Epidaurus.
  - **When to Visit:** April to October for theater performances.
  - **Opening Hours:** Ancient Theater: 8:00 AM - 8:00 PM.

- **Contact Info:** +30 2753 022280, [Official Website](http://www.epidavros.gr)
- **Hidden Gems:** The Tholos of Epidaurus, a circular building with intriguing architecture.

22. Aegina:

- **General Details:** Aegina, a day trip from Athens, unfolds its pistachio orchards and ancient wonders. The Temple of Aphaia and the Monastery of Saint Nectarios beckon exploration. Best visited from March to October, Aegina's Marathonas Beach offers a tranquil escape, while the island's vibrant atmosphere immerses visitors in local life.
- **Key Attractions:** Temple of Aphaia, Aegina Town, Monastery of Saint Nectarios.
- **When to Visit:** March to October for pleasant weather.
- **Contact Info:** +30 2297 023192, [Official Website](http://www.aegina.gr)
- **Hidden Gems:** Marathonas Beach, a peaceful spot with crystal-clear waters.

23. Naxos:

- **General Details:** Naxos, the largest Cycladic island, invites exploration of ancient ruins, charming villages, and beautiful beaches. Portara's iconic gate and Chora's labyrinthine streets reveal the island's historical richness. Best enjoyed from May to October, Naxos balances ancient mythology with contemporary delights, offering a diverse tapestry of Greek island life.

- **Key Attractions:** Portara, Chora Old Town, Apollo Temple.

- **When to Visit:** May to October for beach weather.

- **Contact Info:** +30 2285 22363, [Official Website](http://www.naxos.gr)

- **Hidden Gems:** Apollonas Village, a serene coastal village with a Kouros statue.

24. Kastoria:

- **General Details:** Kastoria, embraced by a serene lake, whispers tales of Byzantine and Ottoman influences. The lakeside setting and Dragon's Cave showcase the town's natural beauty. Best explored from April to October, Kastoria's Byzantine Museum and Doltso's historic district offer glimpses into the town's rich heritage, creating an idyllic escape into Greek history and culture.

- **Key Attractions:** Kastoria Lake, Byzantine Museum of Kastoria, Dragon's Cave.

- **When to Visit:** April to October for milder temperatures.

- **Contact Info:** +30 2467 062265, [Official Website](http://www.kastoria.gr)

- **Hidden Gems:** Doltso, a historic district with well-preserved mansions.

Essential Information

Currency:
- Greece operates with the Euro (€) as its official currency, ensuring convenient transactions for travelers. ATMs are readily available at airports, transportation hubs, and throughout cities and towns. Credit cards are widely accepted in hotels and restaurants, providing flexibility in payment methods.

Language:
- The official language of Greece is Greek. While English is commonly spoken in major tourist areas, especially by the younger population, familiarizing yourself with a few basic Greek phrases enhances your travel experience and fosters connections with locals.

Visas:
- Greece generally does not require a visa for stays up to 90 days for most travelers. European Union (EU) nationals typically have visa-free access. However, certain nationalities may need a Schengen visa, so it's crucial to verify specific requirements before your journey.

Money:
- Greece's extensive network of ATMs facilitates easy access to cash, available at airports, transportation hubs, and urban areas. Major hotels and restaurants widely accept credit cards, ensuring convenient and secure transactions.

Mobile Phones:
- European and Australian mobile phones typically function in Greece. Travelers from other regions should activate roaming on their devices. To make local calls more cost-effective, consider purchasing a local SIM card upon arrival.

Time:
- Greece operates on Eastern European Time (EET), which is GMT/UTC plus two hours. Being aware of the time difference is helpful when scheduling activities or making travel arrangements.

Room Tax:

- Visitors should be mindful of a potential 'room occupancy tax,' typically ranging from €1 to €5 per night. Specific details can be found in local accommodations or on official tourism websites.

Seasons:

- Greece experiences distinct seasons, each offering unique advantages:

- High Season (Jul–Aug): Expect crowds at major attractions, especially during August. Prices may rise during holidays. Late December through March is considered high season in mountainous areas.

- Shoulder Season (Apr–Jun & Sep–Oct): Ideal for budget-conscious travelers, with more favorable accommodation prices. Spring boasts festivals and blooming flowers, while autumn offers pleasant weather and the grape harvest.

- Low Season (Nov–Mar): Traveling during this period can save up to 30% compared to high season rates. Some sights and hotels may be closed, making it an excellent time for cultural events in major cities.

Emergency Numbers:

- In case of emergencies, remember these vital contact numbers in Greece:

  - Ambulance: 166
  - Police: 100
  - Fire: 199

- When calling from outside Greece, dial your international access code, followed by Greece's country code (%30), and then the number (including the '0').

Useful Websites:

- While in Greece, take advantage of these online resources:

  - *Hellenic Railways Organization (www.trainose.gr):* Official website for train travel information.

  - *Ekdromi (www.ekdromi.gr):* A guide to rural accommodations, offering a unique lodging experience.

  - *Greek Gastronomy Guide (www.greekgastronomyguide.gr):* Explore local producers, restaurants, and markets, immersing yourself in Greece's culinary delights.

- *Visit Greece (www.visitgreece.gr):* The official Greek National Tourism Organization website, providing comprehensive travel information and resources for your Greek adventure.

Daily Costs:

- Budget (Less than €100):

- Traveling on a budget offers cost-effective options in Greece. Expect to pay around €15-30 for a hostel dorm bed and between €50 and €110 for double rooms in budget hotels. Meals at local eateries are generally affordable, with prices for traditional dishes ranging from €6 to €12.

- Midrange (€100–€250):

- Midrange options provide good value, with double rooms in hotels typically costing between €110 and €200. Enjoying lunch and dinner at local restaurants may cost approximately €25 to €50 per meal, and admission to attractions usually ranges from €4 to €15.

- Top End (More than €250):

- Travelers seeking luxury can explore a range of options, with double rooms in upscale hotels ranging from €200 to €450. Dining at high-end restaurants may cost between €50 and €150 per person, offering exceptional culinary experiences. Enjoying cultural events, such as theater performances, might cost between €40 and €200.

Opening Hours:

- Opening hours in Greece vary by season, with high-season hours generally applying from April to September or October, and low-season hours from October or November to March. It's essential to note that these hours may decrease during the shoulder and low seasons.

- General opening hours:
   - *Banks: 8.30am–2.30pm, Monday to Friday*
   - *Restaurants: noon–3pm and 7pm–11pm*
   - *Cafes: 8am–10pm*
   - *Bars and clubs: 9pm–3am*

- *Shops: 9am–9pm, Monday to Saturday*

Arriving in Greece:

  - Depending on your destination in Greece, you'll likely arrive at one of the major airports. Here are some key transportation options from a few major airports to city centers:

    - *Eleftherios Venizelos Airport (Athens):* Options include the metro for €10 (departing every 30 minutes from 6.30am to 11.30pm), a bus for €6 (running every 15-20 minutes from 6.00am to midnight), or a taxi with a set fare of €38 (approximately 40 minutes).

    - *Macedonia Airport (Thessaloniki):* Choose between a bus for €2 (departing every 30 minutes from 5.30am to 11.30pm) or a taxi with a set fare of €20 (around 30 minutes).

    - *Nikos Kazantzakis Airport (Heraklion, Crete):* Options include a bus for €1.70 (departing every 15-20 minutes from 6.00am to 11.00pm) or a taxi with a set fare of €25 (approximately 20 minutes).

    - *Diagoras Airport (Rhodes):* Choose between a bus for €2.50 (running every 20-30 minutes from 6.30am to 11.30pm) or a taxi with a set fare of €25 (around 30 minutes).

With this practical guide, you're well-equipped to immerse yourself in the wonders of Greece, embracing its rich culture, historical marvels, and breathtaking landscapes.

First Time in Greece?

What to Wear:

- Greece, with its diverse landscapes and cultural richness, also carries a distinct fashion sense. While Athens may lean towards a blend of casual and chic, the islands embrace a more relaxed style. In cosmopolitan areas, men often opt for smart-casual attire, while women may choose light dresses, skirts, or comfortable trousers. Casual wear, including shorts, T-shirts, and sandals, is suitable for beach excursions. When exploring historical sites, sturdy footwear is recommended. Spring and autumn may call for layers, including a light jacket for cooler evenings.

Sleeping:

- Planning your stay in advance is wise, especially during peak seasons or in popular destinations. Consider these accommodation options:
    - **Hotels:** Greece offers a wide array of hotels, ranging from luxury establishments to budget-friendly choices.
    - **Traditional Guesthouses:** Embrace Greek hospitality in quaint guesthouses, showcasing local charm and authenticity.
    - **Villas:** Ideal for families or larger groups, villas provide a private and comfortable retreat.
    - **Island Inns:** Experience the unique atmosphere of family-run inns, often nestled in picturesque island settings.
    - **Hostels:** Affordable and social, hostels cater to budget-conscious travelers, with shared or private room options.

What to Pack:

- Ensure a delightful and comfortable exploration of Greece by packing the following essentials:

- Comfortable walking shoes for cobblestone streets and exploration.
- Sun protection essentials: hat, sunglasses, and sunscreen.
- Electrical adapter for charging devices.
- A hearty appetite for savoring Greek gastronomy.
- Stylish yet casual clothing for blending in with the locals.
- Patience to navigate occasional delays with a relaxed attitude.
- A phrasebook to engage with locals and enhance your experience.

Money:

- Greece embraces a variety of payment methods, with credit and debit cards widely accepted. Visa and MasterCard are commonly recognized, though American Express may have limited acceptance. ATMs are easily accessible, but it's advisable to be mindful of potential transaction fees. Experimenting with multiple ATMs can be prudent if your card is initially rejected.

Bargaining:
- While bargaining is customary in markets, it's generally discouraged in regular stores. In smaller, artisanal shops, especially in the southern regions, good-natured bargaining might be acceptable, particularly if making multiple purchases.

Tipping:
- Tipping etiquette varies, but here are some general guidelines:
- Taxis: Tipping is optional, often rounding up to the nearest euro.
- Restaurants: Some establishments include a service charge, while others may not. If not included, a small tip is appreciated.
- Bars: Tipping is customary, especially if drinks are brought to your table.

Etiquette:

- Greek society values formality, and understanding local customs enhances your experience:

- Greetings: Greet strangers with a warm "kalimera" (good morning) or "kalispera" (good evening). Handshakes are common, and a friendly demeanor is appreciated.

- Asking for help: Use "signomi" (excuse me) to get someone's attention and "parakalo" (please) when seeking permission or assistance.

- Respect for Culture: When visiting religious sites, dress modestly by covering shoulders, torsos, and thighs. Show respect for local customs and traditions, especially in more conservative areas.

Embark on your first journey to Greece with these insights, allowing you to embrace the diversity, history, and warm hospitality of this captivating destination.

Itineraries

Aegean Odyssey - 2 Weeks

Athens to Santorini

Embark on a two-week Aegean adventure, commencing in the historical city of Athens. Spend the initial days exploring iconic landmarks such as the Acropolis and the ancient Agora. Immerse yourself in the vibrant Plaka district and savor traditional Greek cuisine.

Next, set sail for the mesmerizing island of Santorini. Witness the stunning sunsets over the caldera, stroll through the narrow streets of Oia, and relax on the distinctive black sand beaches. Delve into the island's rich history with visits to ancient Thera and the Akrotiri archaeological site.

Island-Hopping Extravaganza - 3 Weeks

Crete, Rhodes, and Mykonos

Embark on a three-week island-hopping extravaganza, starting in the largest of the Greek islands, Crete. Explore the ancient ruins of Knossos, hike the Samaria Gorge, and relax on the picturesque beaches of Elafonissi.

Continue your journey to the medieval charm of Rhodes. Lose yourself in the narrow streets of Rhodes Old Town, visit the Palace of the Grand Master, and unwind on pristine beaches. Delight in the unique fusion of history and relaxation.

Conclude your odyssey on the vibrant island of Mykonos. Enjoy the lively nightlife, wander through the charming streets of Mykonos Town, and bask in the sun on the island's beautiful beaches. Experience the intersection of tradition and modernity in this Cycladic gem.

Mainland Marvels - 2 Weeks

Thessaloniki to Meteora

Embark on a two-week exploration of the Greek mainland, beginning in the vibrant city of Thessaloniki. Discover the cultural richness of the White Tower, Rotunda, and the city's bustling markets. Indulge in authentic Greek cuisine at traditional tavernas.

Journey to the mystical monasteries of Meteora, perched atop towering rock pillars. Explore this UNESCO World Heritage site, marveling at the stunning landscapes and the religious significance of the monastic complexes. Delve into the local legends and histories that make Meteora a truly enchanting destination.

Peloponnesian Passage - 1 Week

Nafplio, Olympia, and Epidaurus

Embark on a week-long journey through the Peloponnese, starting in the charming town of Nafplio. Wander through its historic streets, visit the Palamidi Fortress, and soak in the seaside atmosphere.

Continue your exploration to the birthplace of the ancient Olympic Games, Olympia. Step back in time as you explore the archaeological site and the Temple of Zeus. Experience the historical significance and athletic spirit of this ancient sanctuary.

Conclude your Peloponnesian adventure in Epidaurus, where the well-preserved ancient theater awaits. Witness ancient performances in this iconic amphitheater, surrounded by the lush landscapes of the region.

These diverse itineraries promise unforgettable experiences, from historical marvels and cultural treasures to the idyllic beauty of the Greek islands. Enjoy your journey through the enchanting landscapes and rich heritage of Greece!

Food and Drinks

The Gastronomic Calendar

Greece's culinary journey is a celebration of seasonal flavors, offering a diverse palette to tantalize your taste buds throughout the year. Explore the unique offerings of Greek cuisine with this overview of the Hellenic culinary calendar:

Spring (March - May)

Spring heralds the arrival of fresh produce, with artichokes, fava beans, and wild greens taking center stage. Traditional Easter dishes, such as lamb and tsoureki, grace tables during festive celebrations. Food festivals like Athens' Dairy Festival and Naxos' Citrus Festival showcase the season's bounty.

Summer (June - August)

As summer unfolds, Greek cuisine bursts with the flavors of ripe tomatoes, cucumbers, and olives. Indulge in the coastal delights of grilled seafood and moussaka. Experience local specialties at events like the Ikaria Food Festival and the Thessaloniki Food Festival, celebrating the best of summer produce.

Autumn (September - November)

Autumn brings a rich tapestry of flavors with the harvest of grapes, figs, and pomegranates. Delight in the earthy aromas of wild mushrooms and chestnuts, especially in regions like Arcadia. Join in the festivities of the Korinthian Cuisine Festival and the Chestnut Festival in Karpenisi.

Winter (December - February)

Embrace the warmth of winter with festive treats like melomakarona and kourabiedes during Christmas. Coastal regions, such as Kavala, offer delectable seafood dishes, including hearty fish stews. Dive into the culinary traditions of the Peloponnese at the Nemean Gastronomy Festival.

Affordable Delights

Souvlaki: Grilled meat skewers, a quick and satisfying street food option.

Spanakopita: Spinach and feta-filled pastry, a flavorful and portable snack.

Koulouri: Sesame-covered bread rings, perfect for a quick breakfast or snack.

Moussaka: Layers of eggplant, minced meat, and béchamel sauce, a hearty and comforting dish.

Gyro: A delicious combination of grilled meat, vegetables, and tzatziki wrapped in pita.

Dakos: Cretan rusk topped with tomatoes, feta, and olive oil, a refreshing appetizer.

Loukoumades: Deep-fried dough balls drizzled with honey, a sweet treat to satisfy your cravings.

Adventurous Tastes

Kokoretsi: Grilled offal wrapped in intestines, a traditional delicacy during Easter.
Taramasalata: A creamy fish roe dip, ideal for seafood enthusiasts.
Patsas: Tripe soup, a hearty dish believed to cure hangovers.
Stifado: Slow-cooked meat stew with onions and spices, a flavorful winter dish.
Horta: Boiled wild greens, a nutritious and earthy side dish.
Fasolada: Bean soup, a staple of Greek cuisine and a symbol of national identity.

Local Culinary Treasures

Greece's culinary landscape is a testament to "filoxenia," the spirit of warm hospitality. Explore the distinctive flavors of various regions:

Crete: Savor the Cretan diet, known for its emphasis on olive oil, fresh vegetables, and aromatic herbs. Try dakos, kalitsounia, and apaki (smoked pork).

Thessaloniki: Delight in the diverse street food offerings, including bougatsa (pastry filled with custard or cheese) and souvlaki. Don't miss local specialties like giouvetsi (baked orzo with meat) and revani (semolina cake).

Santorini: Indulge in the island's unique produce, from cherry tomatoes to white eggplants. Try fava, tomato keftedes, and the renowned Santorinian wine.

Peloponnese: Enjoy the robust flavors of Mani, known for its olive oil, honey, and savory pastries. Dive into Kalamata olives, pasteli (sesame seed bars), and lalaggia (fried dough).

Epirus: Experience the mountainous cuisine with dishes like kontosouvli (rotisserie meat) and tsigaridia (wild greens). Try the famed Metsovo cheeses and warm up with a glass of tsipouro.

Island of Rhodes: Relish the island's gastronomy with moussaka, pastitsio, and the delightful koulouria cookies. Explore the mezedes (appetizers) and fresh seafood along the coast.

Macedonia: Delve into the culinary heritage with dishes like piperopita (pepper pie) and pastrmajlija (flatbread with meat). Enjoy the diverse influences in local specialties such as gyuvetch and tavče gravče.

Embrace the essence of Greek dining by savoring local delicacies, exploring regional specialties, and immersing yourself in the warm hospitality of this culinary paradise. Kali orexi!

Adventure Activities Across Greece

Greece, a country graced with extraordinary landscapes and cultural richness, unfolds as a playground for adventure enthusiasts. From rugged mountainous terrains to azure coastlines, Greece offers an array of exhilarating activities for those seeking an adrenaline rush. In this section, we'll explore the best adventure experiences across the Greek landscape.

Hiking

Embark on a hiking journey through Greece's diverse landscapes. Traverse the dramatic Pindus Mountains, explore the lush Vikos Gorge in Epirus, or venture into the rugged landscapes of Crete's Samaria Gorge. The Peloponnese region boasts captivating trails, while the Cyclades islands provide a unique island-hopping hiking experience. Explore the following locations:

- **Pindus Mountains:** Dramatic landscapes and challenging trails.

- **Vikos Gorge, Epirus:** Lush greenery and one of the deepest gorges in the world.

- Samaria Gorge, Crete: Rugged terrain and unique flora. The best times for hiking are spring and early autumn, offering blooming landscapes and pleasant weather.

Cycling

Discover Greece's diverse terrains on a cycling adventure. Pedal through the Peloponnese Peninsula, conquer the challenging routes of Mount Taygetos, or explore the scenic landscapes of Naxos and Santorini. Urban cycling options include Athens, Thessaloniki, and Rhodes. Explore the following locations:
   - **Mount Taygetos:** Challenging routes with breathtaking views.
   - **Naxos and Santorini:** Scenic landscapes and coastal roads.

Spring and fall are optimal for cycling, with moderate temperatures and vibrant landscapes.

Skiing

While Greece may not be as renowned as other European countries for skiing, it offers excellent opportunities for winter sports. Mainland destinations like Mount Parnassos and Mount Pelion provide skiing options, and the northern regions experience snowfall during the winter months. Explore the following locations:
   - **Mount Parnassos:** Ski resorts with a view of the Gulf of Corinth.

- **Mount Pelion:** Picturesque landscapes for winter sports enthusiasts.

The ski season in Greece runs from December to late March, with January and February being the peak months.

Diving

Explore Greece's underwater treasures through diving activities. The islands, including Crete, Rhodes, and Zakynthos, offer crystal-clear waters and diverse marine life. Discover underwater caves, vibrant coral reefs, and ancient shipwrecks. Explore the following locations:

- **Crete:** Crystal-clear waters and underwater caves.

- **Rhodes**: Diverse marine life and historical wrecks.

The best time for diving is from May to October when the sea temperature is warm, and visibility is optimal.

White-Water Sports

For an adrenaline-pumping experience, head to the rivers of Epirus, especially the Voidomatis River. Engage in white-water activities such as rafting, kayaking, and hydrospeed, surrounded by the stunning landscapes of the Pindus Mountains. Explore the following locations:

- **Voidomatis River, Epirus:** Rafting and white-water adventures.

Spring and early summer provide ideal conditions for white-water adventures.

Rock Climbing

Greece's mountainous regions, including Meteora, Kalymnos, and Mount Olympus, offer diverse rock-climbing opportunities. From limestone cliffs to granite rocks, climbers of all levels can find suitable routes. Explore the following locations:

- **Meteora:** Unique rock formations and challenging climbs.

- **Kalymnos:** Limestone cliffs and a climber's paradise.

The climbing season extends from spring to autumn, providing favorable weather conditions.

Sailing

Embrace Greece's maritime legacy by sailing along its captivating coastlines. Charter a yacht to explore the Cyclades, Ionian, or Dodecanese islands. Discover hidden coves, pristine beaches, and charming fishing villages. Explore the following locations:

- **Cyclades Islands:** Island-hopping adventure with diverse landscapes.

- **Ionian Islands:** Crystal-clear waters and picturesque harbors. The summer months, from June to September, offer ideal sailing conditions with warm temperatures and gentle winds.

Windsurfing

Greece, with its numerous islands and coastal spots, is a windsurfing paradise. Top locations include Rhodes, Naxos, and Paros. Experience the meltemi winds in the Aegean and the consistent breezes in the Ionian Sea. Explore the following locations:

- **Lago di Garda, Rhodes:** Prime windsurfing spot with excellent wind conditions.

- **Naxos and Paros:** Ideal for both beginners and experts.

The best time for windsurfing is during the summer months, ensuring optimal wind conditions.

Best Times to Go

- **Spring (April to June):** Ideal for hiking amidst wildflowers.
- **Summer (July to September):** Perfect for water sports, sailing, and windsurfing without the August crowds.
- **Winter (December to March):** Skiing enthusiasts can enjoy the Greek slopes during these months.

Greece's diverse landscapes, coupled with its rich cultural heritage, provide a playground for adventure seekers. Whether you're drawn to the mountains, the sea, or both, Greece offers a myriad of options for an unforgettable adventure. Seize the opportunity to explore this enchanting country through thrilling activities and experiences. Kaló taxídi!

A brief History of Greece

Ancient Greece: Birth of a Civilization

Ancient Greece, often referred to as the cradle of Western civilization, emerged around the 8th century BCE on the Balkan Peninsula. This period is characterized by the formation of city-states, each with its own distinct government, culture, and identity. Notable city-states include Athens, Sparta, Corinth, and Thebes.

Archaic Period (800-500 BCE): The Archaic Period marked the early stages of Greek civilization. City-states, or "polis," were established, each functioning as an independent political entity. Athens, under the leadership of figures like Solon, initiated democratic reforms, while Sparta adopted a militaristic society.

Classical Period (500-323 BCE): The Classical Period witnessed the zenith of Greek culture and influence. The Persian Wars (490-479 BCE) against the mighty Persian Empire showcased Greek resilience, exemplified by the Battle of Marathon and the Battle of Thermopylae. The Delian League, led by Athens, emerged as a maritime alliance to counter Persian threats.

Golden Age of Athens (460-429 BCE): Athens, particularly during the leadership of Pericles, experienced a cultural and intellectual golden age. This era saw the construction of the Parthenon on the Acropolis, the flourishing of philosophy with figures like Socrates and Plato, and the tragedies of playwrights like Aeschylus and Sophocles.

Peloponnesian War (431-404 BCE): The rivalry between Athens and Sparta culminated in the Peloponnesian War. Sparta, aided by Persian funding, eventually defeated Athens, leading to a decline in the city-state's power and influence. This conflict left Greece weakened, setting the stage for external invasions.

Hellenistic Greece: The Confluence of Cultures

Following the Peloponnesian War, Greece entered the Hellenistic period, marked by the spread of Greek influence throughout the known world. This era, which began with the conquests of Alexander the Great, saw a blending of Greek, Persian, Egyptian, and other cultures.

Alexander the Great (356-323 BCE): Alexander, a student of Aristotle, embarked on an unprecedented military campaign that resulted in the creation of one of the largest empires in history. His conquests extended from Greece to Egypt, Persia, and as far east as the Indian subcontinent. The city of Alexandria in Egypt became a center of culture and learning.

Hellenistic Kingdoms: After Alexander's death, his empire was divided among his generals, leading to the formation of the Seleucid, Ptolemaic, Antigonid, and other Hellenistic kingdoms. These kingdoms continued to disseminate Greek culture while assimilating local traditions.

Cultural Achievements: The Hellenistic period contributed significantly to art, science, and philosophy. The famous mathematician Euclid laid the foundations of geometry, and Archimedes made groundbreaking contributions to mathematics and physics. Hellenistic art, with its emphasis on realism, reflected a departure from the idealized forms of classical Greek art.

Roman Greece: From Conquest to Byzantine Rule

The Roman Republic's expansion brought it into direct conflict with the Greek world, leading to the eventual incorporation of Greece into the Roman Empire. This period, characterized by both Roman influence and the persistence of Greek culture, laid the groundwork for the Byzantine era.

Roman Conquest (146 BCE): The Roman legions, led by generals such as Lucius Mummius, defeated the Achaean League, marking the end of Greek independence. The sacking of Corinth symbolized Rome's dominance in the region. Greece became a province of the Roman Republic.

Pax Romana and Greek Culture: Despite political subjugation, Greek culture thrived under Roman rule. The period of Pax Romana (27 BCE–180 CE) brought stability, allowing the continuation of artistic, literary, and philosophical endeavors. Roman elites admired Greek literature and philosophy, fostering a synthesis of the two cultures.

Christianity's Emergence: The spread of Christianity, originating in the eastern part of the Roman Empire, had profound implications for Greece. The Apostle Paul's missionary journeys brought Christianity to various Greek cities, contributing to the region's religious transformation.

Byzantine Greece: Christianization, Iconoclasm, and Decline

The Byzantine era in Greece witnessed the consolidation of Christianity, the turbulence of iconoclastic controversies, and the eventual decline of the Byzantine Empire.

Christianization (4th–6th centuries): Byzantine Emperor Constantine the Great played a pivotal role in establishing Christianity as the empire's state religion. The Council of Nicaea in 325 CE solidified key Christian doctrines, influencing the religious landscape of Byzantine Greece. Monasticism flourished, with famous monastic centers like Mount Athos emerging.

Iconoclasm (8th–9th centuries): The Byzantine Empire grappled with the Iconoclastic Controversy, a theological dispute over the use of religious images. The iconoclasts, who opposed the veneration of icons, clashed with iconophiles. The ultimate triumph of the iconophiles had a profound impact on Byzantine art and religiosity.

Slavic and Arab Invasions: The vulnerability of Byzantine Greece became evident during the Slavic and Arab invasions of the 7th and 8th centuries. While some areas experienced significant demographic changes, others retained their Greek character. The theme system, a military-administrative division, was implemented to defend Byzantine territories.

Decline and Crusader Period: The Fourth Crusade (1202–1204) dealt a severe blow to the Byzantine Empire. Crusaders, diverted from their original goal, sacked Constantinople, leading to the establishment of the Latin Empire. Greek principalities emerged, ruled by local despots. The Byzantine Empire's decline continued, culminating in the fall of Constantinople to the Ottoman Turks in 1453.

Ottoman Greece: Centuries of Ottoman Rule and the Struggle for Independence

The Ottoman period in Greece spanned several centuries, characterized by cultural diversity, economic challenges, and, eventually, a fervent desire for independence.

Ottoman Conquest (15th century): The fall of Constantinople in 1453 marked the beginning of Ottoman rule in Greece. The Ottoman Empire, under Sultan Mehmed II, expanded its territories into the Peloponnese, central Greece, and the Aegean islands. Local Greek elites often retained their positions under Ottoman rule.

Economic Challenges: The Ottoman era presented economic challenges for Greece. Heavy taxation and the shift of economic power toward the Ottoman elite strained the Greek population. However, some regions, like Thessaly and Macedonia, experienced relative prosperity due to their agricultural output.

Cultural Diversity: Ottoman Greece was characterized by cultural diversity. Greeks, alongside various ethnic and religious groups, coexisted within the empire. The millet system allowed religious communities a degree of autonomy, contributing to the preservation of Greek Orthodox traditions.

Greek Enlightenment (18th century): The 18th century saw the emergence of the Greek Enlightenment, influenced by Western European ideas. Greek scholars, often educated abroad, began advocating for intellectual and political renewal. Rigas Feraios, a Greek revolutionary and poet, envisioned a future Greek state.

Greek War of Independence (1821–1829): The Greek War of Independence marked a turning point. Spurred by nationalist fervor and inspired by Enlightenment ideals, Greeks rose against Ottoman rule. The struggle gained international attention, with notable figures like Lord Byron supporting the cause. The conflict culminated in the establishment of the independent Greek state in 1830.

Modern Greece: Nation-Building, Wars, and 20th Century Challenges

The modern history of Greece is marked by nation-building efforts, wars, geopolitical shifts, and internal challenges. From its emergence as an independent state to the complexities of the 20th century, Greece's journey reflects a tapestry of triumphs and tribulations.

Formation of the Modern Greek State (19th Century): The establishment of the modern Greek state in 1830 was formalized through the London Protocol, recognizing Greece as an independent and sovereign nation. Otto of Bavaria became the first king, and Athens was chosen as the capital. The new state faced challenges in defining its borders and consolidating its territory.

Expansion and the Balkan Wars (1912–1913): The early 20th century saw Greece participating in the Balkan Wars, aiming to expand its territory. Success in these wars resulted in significant territorial gains, including the annexation of Thessaloniki. However, tensions with former allies and new geopolitical realities would shape the coming decades.

World War I and the Asia Minor Campaign: Greece's involvement in World War I and the subsequent Greco-Turkish War (1919–1922), also known as the Asia Minor Campaign, were transformative. The conflict had profound consequences, leading to population exchanges, territorial losses, and a reevaluation of Greece's political landscape.

Interwar Period and Metaxas Dictatorship: The interwar period in Greece was marked by political instability, coups, and the rise of authoritarianism. Ioannis Metaxas assumed dictatorial power in 1936, introducing a period of censorship and suppression of political opposition. Greece's geopolitical position became increasingly significant as tensions in Europe escalated.

World War II and the Axis Occupation: Greece found itself in the midst of World War II, resisting Axis forces. The Greek-Italian War (1940–1941) and the subsequent German invasion led to a brutal occupation. The resistance movement, primarily led by the National Liberation Front (EAM), played a crucial role in the nation's struggle against occupiers.

Civil War (1946–1949): The aftermath of World War II witnessed internal conflicts, with ideological and political divisions sparking the Greek Civil War. The conflict between government forces and communist insurgents resulted in significant social and political repercussions, shaping Greece's trajectory during the Cold War.

Post-War Reconstruction and Democratic Consolidation: The post-war period saw efforts to rebuild and redefine the Greek state. The Marshall Plan provided crucial aid for reconstruction. Greece underwent a process of democratic consolidation, marked by political stability, economic development, and its entry into NATO in 1952.

Military Junta (1967–1974): The late 20th century brought another period of political turbulence when a group of military officers seized power in a coup in 1967. The military junta, led by Colonel Georgios Papadopoulos, suspended democratic institutions, leading to a repressive regime. The regime's collapse in 1974 marked the restoration of democracy.

Contemporary Greece: Democratic Consolidation, Economic Struggles, and Cultural Renaissance

The latter part of the 20th century and the beginning of the 21st century brought about significant developments for Greece, encompassing democratic consolidation, economic challenges, and a cultural renaissance. This period witnessed the country navigating its role in the European Union, facing economic crises, and contributing to global cultural conversations.

Restoration of Democracy (1974): The fall of the military junta in 1974 marked a pivotal moment in Greek history. Following a period of political turmoil, democratic governance was restored. Konstantinos Karamanlis played a crucial role in shaping the post-junta political landscape, and the new constitution of 1975 reinforced democratic principles.

European Integration: Greece's entry into the European Economic Community (EEC) in 1981 signified a commitment to European integration. The subsequent transformation into the European Union (EU) solidified Greece's place in a supranational entity. The EU membership brought economic benefits, though it also exposed Greece to challenges like the Eurozone crisis.

Economic Challenges and the Eurozone Crisis: The latter part of the 20th century and the early 21st century saw Greece grappling with economic challenges. Participation in the Eurozone exposed vulnerabilities in the Greek economy, leading to a severe debt crisis in 2009. The subsequent austerity measures, bailout packages, and economic reforms defined Greece's economic landscape.

Cultural Renaissance: Greece's cultural contributions continued to thrive in the contemporary period. The realm of literature, arts, and philosophy remained vibrant. Greek literature saw the emergence of new voices, and Greek cinema gained international acclaim. The preservation of cultural heritage, including archaeological sites and traditions, remained a priority.

Olympic Games 2004: A significant moment in contemporary Greek history was the hosting of the 2004 Summer Olympics in Athens. The event marked a return to the birthplace of the ancient Olympics and served as an opportunity for Greece to showcase its modern capabilities. The successful organization of the games was a source of national pride.

Social and Political Dynamics: Social and political dynamics in contemporary Greece have been shaped by various factors. Debates over national identity, immigration, and economic policies have been central. Protests and social movements, such as the anti-austerity protests during the Eurozone crisis, underscored the engagement of Greek citizens in shaping their country's trajectory.

Macedonia Naming Dispute: The naming dispute with the newly independent Republic of North Macedonia was a diplomatic challenge for Greece. The issue, centered around the use of the name Macedonia, was resolved with the Prespa Agreement in 2018, showcasing the importance of diplomatic dialogue in the region.

21st Century Challenges: The 21st century posed challenges for Greece, including the global economic downturn, the refugee crisis, and the impact of the COVID-19 pandemic. These challenges tested the resilience of Greek society and prompted discussions about the role of the state, economic policies, and Greece's positioning in global affairs.

Other Useful Information

Accommodation in Greece

Greece, with its rich history, diverse landscapes, and vibrant culture, offers a plethora of accommodation options for travelers. From historical monasteries to seaside villas and modern hotels, Greece caters to a wide range of preferences and budgets. Here's an in-depth guide to help you navigate the diverse world of Greek accommodations:

1. Booking Strategies:

- **High Season Considerations:** Booking in advance is crucial, especially during Greece's high season. Coastal areas buzz with activity in the summer, and popular islands may experience increased demand. Plan ahead to secure your preferred accommodation.

- **Event Timing:** Major cultural or religious events, such as local festivals or religious celebrations, can impact accommodation availability. Check for events in your chosen destination and plan accordingly.

- **Off-Season Benefits:** Bargaining or negotiating for lower rates is more feasible during the off-season. While some tourist facilities may close in the winter, this can be an ideal time for a quieter, budget-friendly Greek experience.

2. Seasonal Rate Dynamics:

- **Peak Tourist Times:** Greece experiences peak tourist seasons during Easter, summer (especially July and August), and the Christmas/New Year period. Accommodation rates may surge during these times.

- **Regional Variations:** Different regions have distinct high seasons. Islands are bustling in the summer, while mountainous areas may attract winter sports enthusiasts during the colder months.

3. Location-Driven Pricing:

- **City vs. Rural:** A midrange choice in a rural area might be more budget-friendly than a budget option in Athens or Thessaloniki. Consider regional variations when budgeting for your trip.

   ### 4. Meal Packages and Board Options:
   - **Half-Board and Full Board:** Some accommodations offer meal packages, including breakfast, lunch, or dinner. Understanding these options can enhance your travel experience, especially if you prefer the convenience of inclusive packages.

   ### 5. Bargaining Strategies:
   - **Low Season Negotiations:** In the off-season, particularly in less touristy areas, attempting to negotiate lower rates is a viable strategy. Longer stays may also open doors for discounted deals.
   - **Last-Minute Deals:** Explore last-minute deals on online platforms like Booking.com, Lastminute.com, and other reputable sites for potential discounts.

Accommodation Types in Greece:

   ### 1. Boutique Guesthouses (Pensioni):
   - **Diverse Settings:** Boutique guesthouses, often referred to as pensioni, can be found in both urban centers and idyllic rural settings. The ambiance ranges from seaside bungalows to rooms in historic city mansions.
   - **Pricing:** Prices can vary widely, ranging from €30 to €100 per person. These guesthouses provide a personalized and often culturally immersive experience.

   ### 2. Camping Adventures:
   - **Well-Equipped Campgrounds:** Greece boasts numerous well-equipped campgrounds, especially in scenic locations. Prices fluctuate with the season, peaking in July and August. Some sites offer all-inclusive rates, while others charge separately for amenities.

- **Resources:** Local tourist offices and online platforms like Campeggi.com, Camping.it, and international services like Eurocamp provide comprehensive campground lists.

3. Monastic Retreats:
- **Spiritual Accommodation**: Some monasteries and convents in Greece offer accommodations to tourists. While early curfews may apply, the experience is unique, and prices are generally reasonable.
- **Resources:** Websites like MonasteryStays.com and local church websites can provide information on available options.

4. Youth Hostels (Ostelli per la Gioventù):
- **Association Affiliation:** Hostels in Greece, known as "ostelli per la gioventù," are often affiliated with Hostelling International (HI). A valid HI card is usually required.
- **Dormitory Rates:** Dormitory beds typically range from €16 to €30, and some hostels offer additional meal packages. Private rooms are available at higher prices.
- **Modern Facilities:** Many hostels have evolved, with fewer restrictions compared to the past, making them suitable for various travelers.

5. Hotels and Pensions:
- **Grading System:** Greece employs a star rating system for hotels, ranging from one to five stars. Prices can vary based on location, season, and quality.
- **Local Assistance:** Local tourist offices and online booking services can assist in finding suitable hotel or pension accommodations.

6. Mountain Hut Retreats:
- **Alpine Getaways:** Greece's mountainous regions, including the Alps and the Apennines, feature rifugi (mountain huts) open from July to September. Advance booking is crucial, and accommodations often include breakfast and dinner.
- **Ownership:** The Club Alpino Italiano (CAI) is a significant operator of mountain huts in Greece.

7. Rental Accommodations:
- **City Challenges:** Finding rental accommodation in major cities can be competitive, with higher rates for short-term

leases. Prices for small apartments or studios near city centers may hover around €1000 per month.

- **Online Platforms:** Websites like Guest in Greece, Homelidays, and Holiday Lettings offer a variety of rental options for short-term stays.

8. Seaside Villas:

- **Scenic Retreats:** Villa rentals in Greece have gained popularity. Agencies like Hellenic Realty, Greek Villas 4 Rent, and Blue Villas offer a range of properties near beaches or medieval towns.

- **Diverse Locations:** Villas are scattered throughout the country, providing a tranquil retreat with proximity to cultural landmarks.

9. Government Accommodation Tax:

- **Tassa di Soggiorno:** Greece introduced an accommodation tax. The "tassa di soggiorno" may result in an additional charge of €1 to €5 per night per room. Exemptions for children may apply, varying by location.

Conclusion:

- **Flexibility and Variety:** Greece's accommodation options provide travelers with flexibility and a variety of experiences. Whether you seek cultural immersion, seaside tranquility, or mountain adventures, Greece has a place for every traveler.

Navigating the spectrum of Greek accommodations enhances your travel experience, allowing you to tailor your stay to your preferences and create lasting memories in this historically and culturally rich destination.

Customs Regulations in Greece

When embarking on a journey to Greece, it is crucial to acquaint yourself with the customs regulations, duty-free allowances, and practical information that will facilitate a seamless travel experience. Here's an in-depth overview tailored to the customs landscape in Greece:

Duty-Free Sales in the EU:

In line with EU regulations, duty-free sales within the European Union are not applicable. Nevertheless, travelers can explore tax-free shopping opportunities at Greek airports, presenting a convenient avenue for acquiring items like fragrance, electronics, and luxury goods.

Duty-Free Allowances for Visitors from Non-EU Countries:

Travelers arriving in Greece from non-EU countries enjoy duty-free allowances, permitting the import of specific items without duties. The allowances include:

- *Spirits: 1 liter (or 2 liters of wine)*
- *Perfume: 50 grams*
- *Eau de Toilette: 250 milliliters*
- *Cigarettes: 200*
- *Other Goods: Up to a total value of €175*

Items exceeding these limits must be declared upon arrival, with the appropriate duty payment required. For substantial purchases, non-EU citizens departing the EU have the option to reclaim value-added tax, presenting an opportunity for savings on significant acquisitions.

Discount Cards:

Greece extends various discount options for travelers, enhancing the affordability of exploration:

- Age-Based Discounts: Visitors under 18 and over 65 may benefit from free admission to numerous galleries and cultural sites. Those aged 18 to 25 often qualify for a 50% discount, with occasional variations for EU citizens.

- Special Discount Cards: Certain cities or regions issue special discount cards. For instance, the Athens Pass may offer complimentary public transport and reduced or free entry to museums. Across Greece, combination tickets provide access to multiple attractions at a more economical rate than individual admissions.

- International Discount Programs: The International Student Identity Card (ISIC) and European Youth Card furnish students and youths with access to discounts on accommodations, museums, dining, shopping, and transportation. These cards are obtainable from recognized travel agencies worldwide.

Electricity:

Navigating the electrical standards is pivotal for any traveler. In Greece:

- Electricity adheres to the European norm of 220-230V with a frequency of 50Hz.

- Wall outlets are typically configured to accommodate plugs with two or three round pins, with the latter grounded and the former ungrounded.

Embassies & Consulates:

Access to embassy and consulate information is indispensable for travelers seeking assistance. Here are contacts for selected embassies and consulates in Greece:

- Australian Embassy/Consulate: Athens
- Austrian Embassy/Consulate: Athens
- Canadian Embassy: Athens
- French Embassy/Consulate: Athens, Thessaloniki, and Heraklion
- German Embassy/Consulate: Athens and Thessaloniki
- Irish Embassy: Athens
- Japanese Embassy/Consulate: Athens
- Dutch Embassy/Consulate: Athens and Thessaloniki
- New Zealand Embassy/Consulate: Athens
- Slovenian Embassy/Consulate: Athens
- Swiss Embassy/Consulate: Athens
- UK Embassy/Consulate: Athens and Thessaloniki
- US Embassy/Consulate: Athens and Thessaloniki

This comprehensive information equips travelers with the knowledge needed to navigate customs regulations, leverage available discounts, and seek assistance through embassies and consulates in Greece. It serves as an invaluable resource, ensuring a well-prepared and enjoyable travel experience in this captivating Mediterranean destination.

Navigating Finances in Greece

When embarking on your Greek adventure, having a solid grasp of the local currency and practical financial considerations is paramount. Here's an extensive guide to money matters in Greece:

Currency:

Greece operates on the Euro (€) as its official currency. Euro banknotes are issued in denominations of €500, €200, €100, €50, €20, €10, and €5. Coins come in €2 and €1, as well as 50, 20, 10, 5, 2, and 1 cents.

ATMs & Credit Cards:

- **ATMs (Automated Teller Machines):** You'll find ATMs, known as Bancomats, widely accessible in Greece. International credit and debit cards bearing the relevant network logo can be used at these ATMs.

- **Credit Cards:** Major credit cards such as Visa and MasterCard are widely accepted. Additionally, cards like Cirrus and Maestro are commonly recognized. While some banks may provide cash advances over the counter, ATMs offer a more practical solution.

- **Card Usage:** Credit and debit cards are suitable for various transactions, including hotel payments, restaurant bills, shopping, supermarket purchases, and toll booth payments.

- **Bank Charges:** Check with your bank regarding foreign transaction charges. Most banks levy a fee of around 2.75% for each foreign transaction, and ATM withdrawals may incur an additional fee, usually about 1.5%.

- **Lost or Stolen Cards:** In the unfortunate event of a lost, stolen, or retained card, promptly contact the issuer to prevent unauthorized usage. Here are the contact details for major card issuers:

  - *American Express (Amex): %800 928391*
  - *Diners Club: %800 393939*
  - *MasterCard: %800 870866*
  - *Visa: %800 819014*

Money Changers:

Currency exchange can be conducted at banks, post offices, or cambio (exchange offices). While banks and post offices typically offer favorable exchange rates, cambio offices may have extended hours. Exercise caution regarding commissions and rates at exchange offices.

Taxes & Refunds:

Greece imposes a value-added tax (VAT), or FPA (Foros Prostithemenis Aksias), at approximately 24% for most goods and services. Non-EU residents can claim a VAT refund on purchases exceeding €120. To secure a refund:

1. Complete a refund form at the point of purchase.
2. Obtain a customs stamp upon departure.
3. Receive an immediate cash refund at major airports, or have it processed back to your credit card.

For further details, visit Tax-Free World Association (www.tfwa.com) or inquire at participating stores.

Tipping:

Tipping customs in Greece are modest compared to some other destinations. While not obligatory, a discretionary tip for exceptional service is appreciated. Here's a general tipping guide:

- **Restaurants:** 5–10% is customary if a service charge is not included.
- **Bars:** For drinks at the bar, leave around €0.50–€1. For table service, 5–10% is reasonable.
- **Hotels:** Tipping €2 for services like porter assistance, maid services, or room service is customary.
- **Taxis:** Round up the fare to the nearest euro.

Postal Services:

Greece's postal system, Hellenic Post (www.elta.gr), is dependable. Stamps (grammata) can be purchased at post offices and authorized vendors. Postage costs vary based on the letter's weight, size, and destination. Priority mail ensures swift delivery within three days to Europe and four to nine days worldwide.

This comprehensive guide equips you with the knowledge needed to effectively manage your finances in Greece, covering currency transactions, taxation, and local tipping practices. It ensures a smooth and informed financial journey throughout your exploration of this captivating Mediterranean destination.

Public Holidays in Greece

Understanding the public holidays in Greece is crucial for travelers, as these celebrations may influence your plans. Here are some of the significant public holidays observed in Greece:
- New Year's Day (Protochronia or Protoselido) - 1 January
- Epiphany (Theofania) - 6 January
- Clean Monday (Kathara Deftera) - February/March
- Independence Day (Doxa i Ohi Day) - 25 March
- Good Friday (Megali Paraskevi) - March/April
- Easter Monday (Deutera tou Pascha) - March/April
- Labour Day (Protomagia) - 1 May
- Whit Monday (Deutera tou Pente) - May/June
- Assumption Day (Dekapentavgousto) - 15 August
- National OXI Day (Ohi Day) - 28 October
- Christmas Day (Christougenna) - 25 December
- Boxing Day (Synaxis ton Agion Anargyron) - 26 December

Keep in mind that Greeks often take their vacations in August, and festivities around 15 August (Assumption Day) can lead to closures of businesses and shops. Plan your travels accordingly to make the most of your experience.

Telecommunication Insights for Greece

Efficient communication is essential during your Greek sojourn. Here are key aspects to consider:

- **Domestic Calls:** Greece has an area code system for telephone numbers. Ensure you are familiar with the area codes, and remember that mobile numbers often start with a three-digit prefix.

- **International Calls:** Opt for cost-effective communication tools like Skype and Viber for international calls. Major cities offer cut-rate call centers for affordable international conversations.

- **Mobile Phones:** Greece operates on the GSM 900/1800 system, compatible with European and Australian phones.

Check your phone's compatibility or unlock it for a Greek SIM card, readily available for tourists.

- **Payphones & Phone Cards:** Payphones in Greece typically accept phone cards, available at post offices, tobacconists, and newsstands. These cards vary in denominations and come with expiration dates. Major providers include Hellenic Telecommunications (OTE).

- **Time Zone:** Greece follows Eastern European Time (EET), which is UTC+2. The country observes daylight-saving time, starting on the last Sunday in March and concluding on the last Sunday in October.

Understanding these telecommunication nuances ensures seamless connectivity during your Greek escapade, allowing you to navigate the rich tapestry of this vibrant Mediterranean destination.

Visas and Residency in Greece

Comprehending the visa and residency landscape is crucial for a well-planned journey to Greece. Here's an extensive overview of the visa and residency regulations for travelers:

1. Schengen Treaty for European Citizens:

   - European citizens hailing from Schengen Treaty countries can enter Greece with a valid identity card or passport.

2. Visa Exemptions for Select Countries:

   - Travelers from various non-EU countries, including Australia, Brazil, Canada, Israel, Japan, New Zealand, and the USA, often enjoy visa exemptions for short-term tourist visits. However, specific conditions and durations may apply.

3. Visas for Non-EU and Non-Schengen Nationals:

   - Non-EU and non-Schengen nationals seeking to stay in Greece for over 90 days or for purposes other than tourism may need specific visas.

   - For detailed and up-to-date information on visa requirements, consult the official website www.mfa.gr or contact a Greek consulate.

4. Residence and Work for EU Citizens:

- EU citizens typically do not require permits to reside or work in Greece. However, after a three-month stay, registration at the local municipal registry office is mandatory. Proof of work or adequate financial means might be requested.

5. Permanent Residence for Non-EU Foreign Citizens:

- Non-EU foreign citizens with five years of continuous legal residence in Greece may apply for permanent residence status.

6. Residence Permits (Blue Certificate):

- Non-EU citizens planning to stay in Greece for over one week at a fixed address should acquire a residence permit, also known as a 'Blue Certificate,' from the local police station.

- Tourists staying in hotels are usually exempt from this requirement.

- The application process for a residence permit can be intricate, necessitating specific documents. Check the official website www.astynomia.gr for the latest requirements under 'Foreign nationals.'

7. Study Visas:

- Non-EU citizens intending to pursue studies at a Greek educational institution must apply for a study visa at the nearest Greek embassy or consulate.

- Essential documents include proof of enrollment, fee payment, and adequate funds to sustain oneself during the study period.

- Study visas align with the study duration and can be renewed within Greece with proof of ongoing enrollment and financial stability.

Understanding these visa and residency intricacies is pivotal for a seamless and legally compliant stay in Greece. Stay updated with official sources to ensure a hassle-free exploration of this captivating Mediterranean destination.

Travelling to Greece

Embarking on a journey to Greece opens up a world of diverse transportation options, ensuring accessibility from various corners of the globe. Greece is intricately connected by air, land,

and sea, facilitating travelers to reach their chosen destinations with ease.

By Air:

Greece boasts several major international airports, with Athens International Airport Eleftherios Venizelos and Thessaloniki Airport being primary gateways. Heraklion International Airport in Crete also handles international flights. A multitude of airlines, both Greek and international, including Aegean Airlines and Olympic Air, offer connectivity.

Intra-European flights are plentiful, serving numerous Greek cities. Renowned carriers like Lufthansa, British Airways, Air France, and KLM operate alongside budget airlines such as Ryanair and Volotea, providing affordable travel options within Greece.

Entering the Country:

- European Union citizens can enter Greece with their national identity card. Other nationalities typically require a valid passport and may need to complete a landing card, especially at airports.

- Greek law mandates carrying a passport or ID card at all times, essential for police registration during hotel check-ins.

- Although land borders usually don't involve passport checks, occasional customs controls, particularly at the border with Turkey, may occur.

By Land:

Greece maintains well-established road and rail links with neighboring countries, particularly in the northern regions. Key border crossings include:

- **Bulgaria**: Accessible routes include Kulata to Promachonas via E79 and Kapitan Andreevo to Ormenio via E85.

- **North Macedonia:** Cross from Gevgelija to Evzoni via A1/E75.

- **Albania:** Enter from Kakavia to Ioannina via E65.

- **Turkey:** Border crossings include Ipsala to Kipi via E90 and Uzunkopru to Kipoi via E87.

By Bus:

Buses offer a budget-friendly travel option, connecting Greece with neighboring countries. Companies like KTEL provide services to major cities, including Thessaloniki and Athens. While less frequent than trains, buses are an economical choice for exploring Greece.

By Car and Motorcycle:
- Vehicles crossing borders should display their country of registration's nationality plate.
- Carry proof of vehicle ownership and third-party insurance. EU-registered vehicles usually have adequate coverage. Consider a European Breakdown Assistance policy.
- Greece's scenic roads are ideal for motorcycle touring, with helmets and a valid motorcycle license mandatory.

By Train:
Greece's railway network facilitates excellent connections with neighboring countries. Regular trains operate between Greece, Bulgaria, North Macedonia, and Turkey. Train travel, particularly for shorter distances, offers an eco-friendly alternative to flying.

By Sea:
Situated amidst the Mediterranean, Greece is intricately linked by ferry services to various countries. Numerous routes, especially during the summer, connect Greece with Italy, Turkey, and other Mediterranean destinations. Vehicle transport prices vary based on size.

For detailed ferry service information, visit websites like [greekferries.gr](https://www.greekferries.gr) and [ferryhopper.com](https://www.ferryhopper.com). Renowned ferry companies serving Greece include Blue Star Ferries, ANEK Lines, Minoan Lines, Hellenic Seaways, and others.

Embark on your Greek adventure with an array of transportation choices, ensuring a seamless and unforgettable exploration of this captivating destination.

Getting Around Greece

Upon your arrival in Greece, a plethora of transportation options awaits, facilitating seamless navigation through the country's captivating landscapes. Greece's extensive network includes trains, buses, ferries, and domestic flights, ensuring convenient travel for every adventurer.

By Air:

While in Greece, domestic flights offer a swift means of travel. The primary carrier for domestic flights is Aegean Airlines, providing efficient connections. Domestic flight prices can range from €50 to €150, depending on the route and time of booking.

By Bicycle:

Cycling enthusiasts will find Greece to be a haven for exploration. Whether bringing your own bicycle or renting locally, the country's scenic routes unfold a mesmerizing journey. Rental prices for bicycles range from €10 to €30 per day, while guided cycling tours can cost between €50 and €100.

By Boat:

Exploring Greece's islands, like Crete and Rhodes, is a maritime adventure. Opt for large ferries or smaller ferries (traghetti) and hydrofoils (aliscafi) for passengers. Major embarkation points include Piraeus, Rafina, and Thessaloniki. Ferry prices vary based on the route and type of ferry, ranging from €20 to €60 for passenger ferries and higher for those carrying vehicles.

By Bus and Metro:

Greek cities boast extensive bus and metro systems, providing reliable urban transportation. Major cities like Athens and Thessaloniki feature well-established metro networks. Bus tickets typically cost €1.20 to €2, while metro tickets range from €1.40 to €2, offering a cost-effective way to explore cityscapes.

By Taxi:

Taxis are readily available at transportation hubs, and radio taxis can be called for added convenience. Keep in mind that the meter starts upon calling, not at the pickup location. Taxis provide a convenient option for short-distance travel within cities, with fares starting around €3 and an additional €1.50 to €2 per kilometer.

By Train:

Efficient and affordable, Greece's trains offer various services, including Regional/interregional trains, InterCity (IC) trains, and high-velocity trains. Tickets and reservations can be made through the Hellenic Railways Organization (OSE) website or at railway stations. Train ticket prices vary, with regional trains starting at €5 and higher-speed trains ranging from €20 to €50.

By Car:

For those who prefer driving, Greece's well-developed road network, including highways and dual-carriageway roads, provides accessibility. Tolls apply on motorways (autostrade). Rental car prices range from €20 to €50 per day, excluding fuel costs. Familiarize yourself with driving nuances, including ZTL zones in city centers.

By Motorcycle and Scooter:

Embrace the popular mode of transport in Greece—motorcycles and scooters. Available for rent in many cities, they offer flexibility for navigating urban areas. Rental prices vary, with scooters starting at €15 per day, while motorcycles can range from €25 to €50 per day.

Conclusion:

Greece beckons explorers with its diverse landscapes, ancient history, and delectable cuisine. Whether venturing through historic cities, idyllic countryside, or sun-kissed coasts, Greece's extensive transportation system ensures a memorable and enriching experience. Uncover the secrets of this enchanting destination, where friendly locals and well-connected routes await your discovery, offering a range of options to suit different budgets.

Copyright and Disclaimer:
© 2023 Luca Petrov. All rights reserved.
Images Source:
Pixbay: (https://pixabay.com/)
All images' rights belong to their respective owners.
For detailed image licensing terms and conditions, kindly refer to the respective image sites' licensing terms and conditions.
Disclaimer:
This disclaimer is hereby presented to inform users of the "Greece Travel Guide" (henceforth referred to as "the Guide") of the terms and conditions of its use. By accessing or using this travel guide, you agree to the following conditions:

1. General Information: The Guide is created for informational purposes and offers travel-related content and advice related to Greece. It aims to provide general information and suggestions, which may not always be up to date. It is not a substitute for professional travel advice.

2. Accuracy of Information: While we strive to provide accurate and current information, we make no representations or warranties of any kind, expressed or implied, about the completeness, accuracy, reliability, suitability, or availability of the information, products, services, or related graphics contained in the Guide. Users should verify information independently before relying on it.

3. Liability Disclaimer: The author and the publisher of this Guide will not be liable for any loss or damage, including but not limited to indirect or consequential loss or damage, or any loss or damage whatsoever arising from loss of data or profits arising out of, or in connection with, the use of this Guide.

4. Third-Party Content: The Guide may include links to third-party websites or services related to Greece. We have no control over the nature, content, and availability of these sites and services. Inclusion of any links does not imply a recommendation or endorsement of the views expressed within them.

5. Safety and Legal Compliance: It is the user's responsibility to exercise caution, act in accordance with local laws and regulations, and ensure personal safety when engaging in any suggested activities or traveling in Greece.

6. Personal Responsibility: Users are solely responsible for their decisions and actions based on the information and advice provided in this Guide. The author and the publisher are not responsible for users' choices or outcomes related to travel or other activities in Greece.

By accessing or using this Greece Travel Guide, you agree to be bound by this disclaimer. If you disagree with any part of these terms and conditions, you are not allowed to use this Guide.

Milton Keynes UK
Ingram Content Group UK Ltd.
UKHW020840301123
433406UK00011B/139